A. N. Irvano was born in 1990
The author has published three novels and one book of
short fiction. This is the author's first book of poetry.

FALLING
HORSE BOOKS

Falling Horse Books

QUARRELS TO BE QUELLED

A Book of Poetry by

A.N. Irvano

Quarrels to be Quelled: A Book of Poetry
Falling Horse Books

Copyright © 2014 A. N. Irvano
First Edition
Cover Design: A.N. Irvano

This collection is a work of fiction. Names, characters, places, events, and incidents either are the product of the author's imagination or are used fictiously. The author's use of actual persons (living or dead), places, and characters is incidental to the purposes of the works, and is not intended to disparage any persons named in the work.

ISBN: 978-0-9960346-3-0
Library of Congress
Printed in the United States of America

Dedicated to the one I have loved, for I have woken up and found I do not need to do so, anymore.

-A.

If I should not say I love you then you,
You should not wear your fleshy human armor
For like your skin my words have purpose too
Not merely a shell nor quiet murmur
To gain union of allelles and ardour
For a poorer match than this there are few
Passion for you I refuse to harbor
Even when you sigh to say you knew
Virtues allow me only to be honest and clear
To only you I'll possess them and relinquish that
you're dear.
It is to only you that I want to let these words
infuse
To put your name now gives too many clues to
deduce.

With widows I thought I could empathize
When far from you I have no port
After seeing their heartbreak I will emphasize
This heart has gone through no contort.

Do you have freedom at life's gate
When to death you did tear
All of the good I'll recreate
To make this matter fair
While upwards my hands do stretch
I do not forget to have my feet square
To get the best I can from myself fetch
Not needing to go to any new resort
In times I do need the gate for support

To hold you again is critical
I have fallen on my last resort
It is as though I forgot how historical
We are not a John and his escort
Before I paint us anything too satirical
Or anything like we both abhor
I would like to become metaphorical
Your absence promotes within me fissions
For which I should see physicians
Your place in my heart was of a dynasty
That held absolutely no rivalry
But to you or me to even implicate
The idea of the act to fornicate
I should that there was a fair shame
To which there was only chair or chain

In your green eyes I see more worlds
Than in the ocean I see waves
To leave at your feet gems and pearls
Would be the same as to the Gods I gave
Like moss your mind does twirl
I could never know how it will next behave
I am selfish to want to see your life unfurl
Does that sound like me making a slave
I regret wanting you and count it a stain
On my desires I will keep a shorter rein.

Falling mist from great heights
Lands on ears that want to hear
The way your hair would shift and sound
Whenever you and I slept near.

Please avoid talking to new people as of late
When you do you tend to get nervous, frenetic
With the comfort of no-one near I recreate
To see if the oddity here is genetic
Placing blame on your parents for thinking to date
Hurts my fellow man; no I'll go synthetic
You do poor in the race; this may start at the gate
To this your handlers should be sympathetic
Your teachers, then, are at a downward rate
You will learn to walk your peers' same gait
Without encountering the need for paramedics
If you sing your voice will be your own anesthetic.

Would anything stop your two eyes
From sparkling like waterfalls
Better than my own when they are
Quiet ponds that can't quite recall?

All of the ways a task could be mistaken
Lead to the final and first way to awaken.
Found in the past are answers to unlearn;
Here is a many places to not return
The long-told questions steeped in mirth,
Unable to be solved belong in the earth.

Wandering in my thoughts for innumerable hours
Led me to wonder about you with uncontrolled
powers.
If you're not in my future I'm coming back for
these flowers.
There are metaphors that won't work after being
broken,
Feelings that fall apart whenever bad thinking is
spoken.
I could be convinced to put aside desires
To watch my own body on the funeral pyre.

We are happy to push past the edge
Blind is our flesh of where is the extent
Is is too much to now allege
That I sometimes miss your scent
A perfect picture of you I could sketch
The feeling from your touch is persistent
To the idea of you my entire body will outstretch
My frustrations turn to blocking like a wedge
So to the idea of abstinence I'll bow out
I again want to feel your pleasure throughout.

To the last breath of yours I start a tradition
A place for your passing soul in prayer
There are times when faith goes in remission
Know that of you we are always now aware
You're in a place good enough to fill your whole
cognition

All of this as beautiful as what you could share
From a life you filled with goals and missions
Thoughts of you will not be lost or left in disrepair
For you are worthy enough to emulate--
If only this would help the sadness alleviate

In your life the best emulate
Your goodness leaves no doubt
Day to day your best does escalate
A good reputation is not throughout
Those predecessors did not investigate
Not to make you an object of any flout
Not someone I'd eventually need to abort
But one to stay to receive mutual support
Gemini twists made true the worst doubts
In your life my light won't emanate

To experience life as it is to be analytical
Do not only see others' disapproval
When you experiment being abneural
Gone is every ounce of energy I have spent
I cannot stop when someone else is discontent
I have come to decide my time is not cheap
My path is one that is dangerously steep
I choose to walk a road most would resent
These truths I choose not to let ferment
I choose also friends that don't follow like sheep
Nor let ones in that turn thoughts into creeps
With me don't just strive to keep afloat
But start to thrive enough to gloat

To all past days that I did mistreat
I will lay down my intent to repent
With my actions I will stop the retreat
A change of mind I have underwent
To summarize the change is no small feat
Nor to pin-point any singular event
While excluding names and being discrete
A change of mind makes me want to augment
Times when I should have retreated with terror
Would avoid and circumvent atrocious error.

Like lichen and stone you are attached
To any of those that can play spiritual
To these matters my door may be more closely
latched
The ones you keep close should be more veritable
To you a little better matched
For my view may be only empirical
But they do need to be dispatched

I've noticed those from upstate
do not deviate
when you want to alleviate
 nor not alternate
 they will want to eliminate
 when you want de-escalate
 but you've been decided to date
to be best candidate to decorate
the halls of those that didn't calculate
Enough to be alienated
so don't despair
stay aware
and live off of the evening prayer
to properly calibrate
and assimilate
what is fair and square
before you frustrate
to the point of explicate
and need to implicate.

Simple trials to you as of yet
To do would actually fix the leak
Follow through to avoid the wet
How often do you really pique
Quickly cacheing all of life's debt
To see what havoc you can wreak
This game I don't think you get
I won't show what can detour a few
You had the abilities of ten men
I should have learned before you;
I've been let down quite often.

It has been too long since I've not been upper
But you, you are a definite other
When your body passes me I have adrenaline
Soar, asking to soak in your elements
Imagining you living well but alone
To this I have asked; Gods don't condone
In this I am neither determined
Nor altogether patient
To indiscriminate love I am not inclined
We should both decide now and redefine

Away from me I'd like to distract
The lights you see I will diffract
A sight of me as I react
To whites on you no longer intact
Your blood and teeth will be poor
When they thud and fall on the floor

Making powers of deductions dispatched
And to logic be very strongly attached
More men than you have and they've
All known enough to be of similar brain-wave
Others adjust to becoming categorical
And to flying at the truth by being historical

If my mind would stop growing tired
Of tending to the flowers I will pick
For you until you give them to a buyer.
To see that they grow unperturbed
Defends best against being disturbed.

Insanity in it long detours
That if a cure I could insure
I would stop you from that tour
Of its hallways you'll be no visitor
Particular to what you are insecure

From which I have suffered similar

The tumors that I grew I looked for

Under the shelves and under the floor
To no longer hear the uproar of inner war
The reason for my peace is really yours

To the purple skies with cloud swirls
Is where I saw the couple, they've
Run off with the dog and cat of the girls
Before they left to them I gave
Oysters shucked without the pearls
Should I have warned them
On how they would be behave
Or let them naively find lovely worlds?

Pouring between the pines the sun is granulate
Though moving the scene is inanimate
Golden sun rods go between branches and float
Reminding me of what make this forest so remote
Seeing my plane resting in the great expanse of
shade
I let the image of the rising sun against pines fade
Each stride across the meadow is a closer gain
To my blue bi-plane.

I know that I've
Gotten hurt enough
To need help to revive
No more playing rough
If I will survive

On you there is nothing to augment
Nothing that is anything but a treat
Your body is beauty to an un-Godly extent
That I wouldn't get caught with you in my sheets
Even to think of you there is disapproval
From the one time I did I still get reproval
I check new thoughts of you at the gate
Because my repulsion to you is total
Even if you are first-rate

I find to day your best does escalate
Such a good reputation is not throughout
Those predecessors to me have a way to rebut
I was not trying to make you an object of flout
Not someone I'd eventually need to abort
But one to stay to receive mutual support
Gemini twists made true the worst doubts
In your life my light won't emanate

My boundaries laid bare
To show how I love and care
I ask your mind to make fair
And to my sanity a prayer
Treat me like a fragile ware

Before doing with your own volition
You must ask first the universal permission
You have power to prize what is in the skies
Beyond the surmised of what it can comprise
Not just with your cognition
Should you go on this mission
Of which your willing transport
Will not let you get lost or abort
Look inwardly instead of acting idly
Speak not rigidly or on what is said allegedly
The universe will calculate what you want to
activate
And either eliminate
Or move to emulate
To come into fruition
That in your cognition

No more to the sky
Than to you do I rely
It is true I improvise
Learning from tries
Not to my surprise
I never caused demise
From what I surmise
I still deserve chastise
If I let my mind buy
Fools' finds not wise
Added-on supplies
All I need I comprise
No more will I explicate
How you frustrate
I willing start to implicate
That we quiet down
And fornicate

The room left bare
Is seen clearly
Without any ware
Is seen ideally

It may be time to signal the ritual
You can be blamed for fraudulent intent
I see you now as being amoral
I'll be the next factor to your descent
Everything after everything is causal
Which leads to event after event
I don't want to wish your events abusal
But I see your feet planted in cement
You seem to like to hear what
To learn before the door's shut
I try to only disambiguate
Not to self-beneficiate
The pain of what will frustrate
Drawn out to soothe and alleviate
On my heart and brain are sprains
But in health they can only gain

I'll leave if to me you aggravate
Just because I won't give in to alternate
Doesn't mean I won't continue to calculate
Find a happier path to assimilate
Grouping of thoughts which you can participate
Not wiled along as a deadly candidate
This allegedly led to Poe's elimination;
People will poison you until you're inarticulate
Acting as only parasitic opportunists
They'll watch your dismemberment escalate
And help the vultures allocate what to plate-
To this side,
away from light,
do not deviate.

The sky hides behind pines
Or, more likely, from mankind
Our lifestyle is unrefined
now can be well times
From being revived
Reform work hives
Where from good derives
The way we thrive
From natural lives
To the pines I withdraw
While friends hee and haw
Donkeys may guffaw
I hold the last hurraw
For my land has my law

With only health intact
I struggle until the last act
When to joy I'll react
By only good I'm backed
Leading to what I attract
Along the path I did veer
To the demons I went near
Of which were insincere
But to them I am no peer
Empathy allows for one tear
That falls on graves of victory
That the demon's be history
They say there is no mystery-
My love was so contradictory
It gave Hell a finalizing injury

The last time I was near
One to me to call a peer
I was not with good gear
Not equipped to be sincere

The little bunny gave birth
A surprise under my bed!
For a mother to come forth
she waited; they died instead.

My mind not yet fully inured
My growth not fully matured
My love not yet made impure
No need for what it is you're
My love not yet made impure
No need for what it is you're
Prescribing for me to cure
I am the teller;
You the seller
You have no life propeller
To find what is stellar

How could you possibly offer
Food when the only affair
I wish you to share
Is for you to tear
My nethers a need for spare
Please make them stretch
A new pair I'd love to sketch
With legs out-stretched
My sweet water may retch-
Not every time that does fetch-
In our bed will be ponds
In which we'll correspond
We will hold our wands
With power that responds

There is a hope that I might
From my solitude take flight
To be guided by friends' might
When to myself I have right
About this I will not fight

I touch the child's cheek
I have known him a week
I touch his cheek with my lips
I hold him by the hips
We both watch the sky
Only I want to die
He needs no fulfillment
Even after his parents' argument
It is the swaying leaves we watch
The moving trees sway and launch
Neither of us talk or initiate it
Until our thoughts are abated.

My thoughts offbeat
Therefor never elite
I see the inherit
Which needs no merit

I find there are times when
All I want is to be alone
And there are times when
All I want is to be at home

My roommate is not home yet
I wonder when the time will be
That my solitude is in the drift net
And I am again with companionship

I check my texts
Not like I used to
Message from my ex
about his own birthday

I have forgotten many facts
Like birthdays and sonnets
More than those it is acts
built of friendship that I have lost

So now when I check my phone
I know there is nothing there for me
Too many friendships have been blown
So I sit in solitude

So I sit in solitude
and think of what I have given up
With disarming magnitude
Through texts and simple spats

So I sit in solitude
Until a friend built of reliance
Will break my lassitude
Like psychiatrist to client

There is no recourse
for the soft falling of bodies
as they slide from home to home
There is no way out
for the people making plans
with people they will not love
There is no vindication
for those those attesting to
love that is indiscriminate
There is no excuse
for the blind eye to indignation
There is no reason for blind love.

Don't exist here
Don't exist where the men
must throw roses
and the women
the women who have been waiting
hands under thighs
lips under teeth
waiting
hoping
dreaming
dreading
to meet a man
To finally fuck a
man into believing
And the men throw
away dignity
for a dream
that doesn't exist
A life detached
from the others' suffrage
A life attached
to the others' pleasures
Contingencies are made in
Copulation and pleasure
and those kill the dream.
And the women don't throw
anything anymore.

There are so many parts of you
That fall prey to the scoundrels inside
But each time I see you like this
Curled up with your sadness and glory
I fall with you and am the happy victim

I had swum well forever
even as a very little girl
swimming beside my mom underwater
in the sapphire haze of swimming pools

I had felt like a whale calf with its mother,
safe from danger.

We used to paint our walls as teenagers
But now we're afraid that some asshole
Won't get the idea or our artistic goal
And they'll paint over it with a white cage

Well here's to the assholes
You make me want to kill myself
And here's to the assholes
I'm afraid to kill myself

Because what if you find out
This town will hold me between
Layers and layers of quilted doubts
To suffocate my pain throughout

I really do want to kill myself
It hurts because I used to stay sane
I used to put my pain on a shelf
But now I don't go against the grain

And maybe that's the problem
I'm so afraid of hurting the assholes
That I don't get up when I've fallen
And I don't proudly paint my walls

Well here's to the assholes
You make me want to kill myself
But you're such an asshole
That I think you'll still feel swell.

Least of all I do not want for you
To come back in my life only to say
Your lack of words I did misconstrue
As you would come back a later day
When it is tonight that my heart spasms
Thrashing inside the cage I have built
Calling upon old friends and assassins
Through my rib's twenty-four sword hilts
Coursing and concerned love is manned
To fight for a love you have not planned.